ANCIENT CHINA

by

C. A. BURLAND

Illustrated by

YVONNE POULTON

HULTON EDUCATIONAL PUBLICATIONS

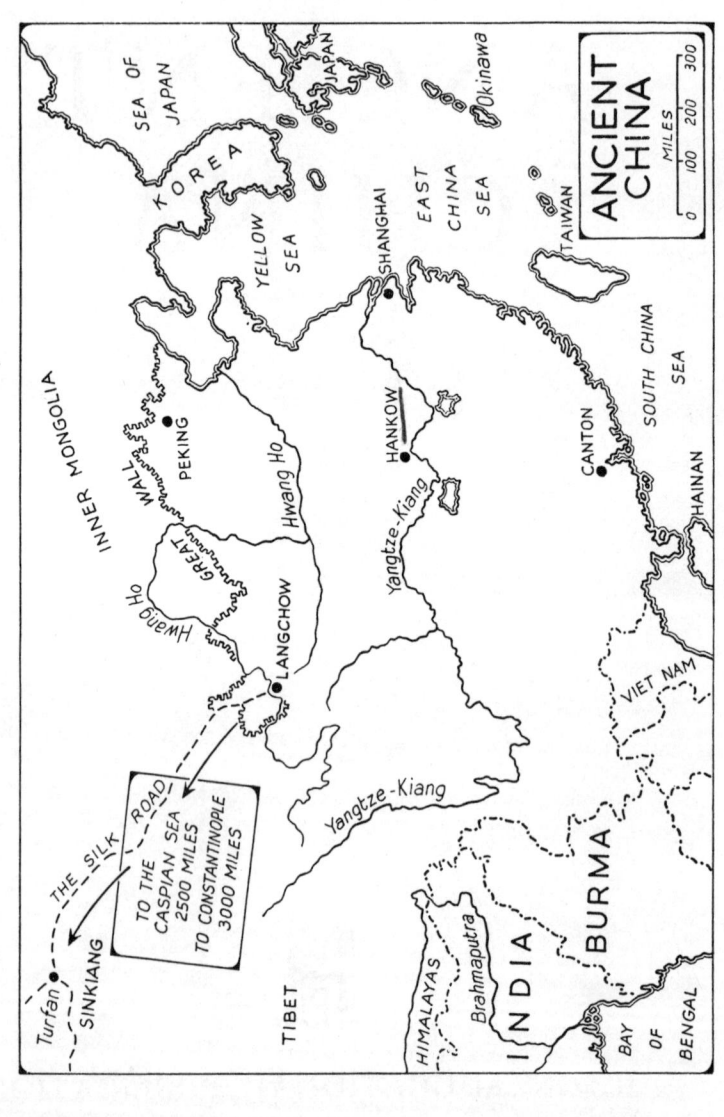

The Country and the People

China is a large country, almost as large as the whole of Europe. Two of the world's longest rivers flow through it—the Yangtze Kiang, 3,500 miles long, and the Hwang Ho, 2,600 miles long. On the East its coastline faces the Pacific Ocean in a great curve of nearly two thousand miles. There are many ranges of high mountains, some of them rich in minerals. In between them the river valleys are fertile and filled with farms. On the north there are great stretches of plain covered with a sandy loess soil. This is excellent grain growing and pasture country. Near the mouths of the two great rivers there are immense lowland plains and delta country, often in danger of flooding, but very fertile.

The climate of such a big country varies a great deal. In the north the winters are severe, with months of heavy snowfall. In the south snow is hardly known. In the west the Central Asian deserts border the country.

The Chinese vary a great deal among themselves. The tall, pale-skinned people of the north appear very different from the wiry, brown people of the south. They all have straight black hair. Their skin is rather thicker than ours. This gives them more protection from cold, but causes them all to look rather yellowish in colour. Their eyelids have a deep fold which makes their eyes seem to slant upwards and outwards. They are mostly a patient, hard-working people who are very proud of their great past. They have always respected learning, and had a love of music, poetry and painting.

Early History

Confucius, the great teacher of China

No one knows when people first came to China. They were primitive hunters at first, but more than five thousand years ago they began to work in metal and build towns. History began in the valleys of the great rivers just where they enter the rich coastal plain. Here great leaders invented the Chinese system of writing by symbols. They discovered how to control the floods, and to irrigate their farms. Then came a period of unified rule under the emperors of the Chou dynasty.

In the latter days of these Chou Emperors the country split up. When the Kings of Assyria were carrying the Jewish people into slavery, the princes of China were listening to the teaching of Kung Fu Tze, whom we know as Confucius.

After the time of the Chou came the period of the Han Dynasty. We know a great deal about the Han because many of their books have survived, and they left records of their life and customs in moulded and painted bricks from which their tombs were made.

But, as the Chinese would say, everything grows and changes. So the Han dynasty became feeble and many of the local Princes rebelled. There followed a period known as The Warring States. For more than two centuries China was divided, but in the end it was brought together by two great emperors of the Sui Dynasty. But the last of these Emperors let his country drift into danger from the tribes of the western plains. China could only be saved by revolt. Then in A.D. 618 the T'ang dynasty was formed and commenced what the Chinese claim to be the greatest and happiest period in all their history.

The great emperors of the T'ang period ruled over many nations. In China itself eight different languages were spoken, but Chinese rule extended over Tibet, and the desert province of Sin-Kiang, and then out to guard the great trade roads to the west. At one time Chinese garrisons guarded the road as far as the Caspian Sea. From time to time the size of the Empire changed. It was impossible to protect the western provinces all the time from raids by Huns and Tartars, and the Turkish tribes of the far west. Sometimes whole provinces were overrun, but in the end order always returned, and the rule of the Emperor was regained.

A border raid by Tartar tribesmen

On the north side there was no threat to the Empire from the primitive hunting tribes of the tundra. Gradually Chinese farmers extended their land towards the north, but only under the pressure of necessity. They disliked leaving their homes in search of new land, even if they needed it to grow enough food.

In the south, Chinese civilisation moved slowly into the tropical mountain jungles. It was never a war of conquest but rather a slow contact with the local tribes who gradually discovered that the Chinese way of life was best.

The Family

Everything in the Chinese civilisation depended upon the Chinese idea of the family. The Emperor was like the father who worked and planned for the good of his family. The wise old counsellors were like the old grandparents. The Ministers of State were the good servants and the Chinese people were the children for whom they cared. They really felt that the whole Empire was a union of friendly families.

The Ancestors came first in the ordinary family at home. They were represented by the carved and painted tablets of wood above the altar in the home. Most

A Chinese family of grandparents, parents and children

families could count back their ancestors for more than a thousand years. Everyone felt that the past members of the family were always an influence in everyday life. Next came the elders . . . grandparents, or perhaps even great-grandparents. However crochety and sour they might be, the children of the house waited on them and cared for them in every way they could. These old people did not rule the house, but they were the wise counsellors to whom the head of the household would come for advice.

12

Father was the head of the household. He earned most of the money and looked after the family business. Mother was the mistress of the household. She first made sure that everybody in the house had enough food. She also looked after the sewing and cleaning. If she was rich, she might have slave girls and paid servants to help her. If she was poor, she would rely on her daughters to help with the cleaning, and on grandmother to do the sewing.

Children

Every Chinese family looked on children as the hope for the future of the family. They were very fond of them, even if some of them were girls who would later marry into other families.

Tiny babies were wrapped up and kept in their cradles. Mother would sometimes take them out bundled up in the back of her gown, so that they could peep over her shoulder.

As soon as they could toddle around, they were dressed like the grown-up people. Their heads were nicely shaved, and little girls grew one long lock of hair, while little boys had three patches of hair left. When it grew long, it was done up into fancy knots tied with

A young mother with the newest baby and her little boy

ribbon. Boys had hoops, kites and toy soldiers to play with. Girls had great fun with their dolls and dolls' houses. They even had toy cooking sets. But most of the time the children ran around with the rest of the family. Until they were about six they spent most of the time with their mothers. After that boys and girls began to do separate little jobs about the house. Girls helped with the cleaning and cooking, and boys collected firewood and helped father at his work.

If they could afford it, the parents sent the bigger boys to school to learn to write and read. Schools were hard, and boys were often beaten with a cane because the teachers thought it was good that they should learn to suffer pain without making a fuss. It was not an easy life for a big boy at school. He usually learnt well in the hope of escaping quickly.

The Chinese thought that a family with many children was a strong family. The boys would carry on the family name, and the girls would be good bargains to exchange in marriage with other families. Of course Chinese families were so ancient that nobody knew how they were related at the beginning of history. So the simple rule was never to marry anyone with the same family name. In China the family name has always been the first name of a person. Kung Fu Tse was a Mr. Kung, whose personal name was Fu Tse.

Eating and Feasting

The Chinese always thought it very bad manners to eat heavily. Their everyday meal was usually very simple, with only two or three courses. Mother would do the cooking, but she would eat separately with her daughters, after father and the men in the family had finished their meal. Perhaps it was just as well, because some of the nicest things could be kept back for the ladies.

Most food was served in little pottery bowls. One dipped a pair of chopsticks into it, seized a small ball of food with them, and threw it into one's mouth. Sometimes a spoon was used for sauces—a narrow elegant

How to eat with Chinese chopsticks

spoon which one pointed towards one's lips and poured just a few drops of tasty soup. Tea was drunk from small bowls with no handles. Two or three tea leaves were dropped in each bowl and boiling water was poured over them. The tea was judged as much by the beauty of its scent as by its flavour. There were many kinds of tea: green, black and red. In T'ang times tea was very fashionable. The tea shrub was thought to have sprung up from the eyelids of a very holy prince who was determined never to sleep. In return for the sacrifice of his eyelids, the tea shrub grew up to bring peace and pleasure to all who used it as their drink.

At great festivals the ceremonious meal might take half a day to eat. There was great care in placing people in their proper social position around the table. Guests would be polite and take positions lower than those they were entitled to, and the host had to lead them politely to their proper position. There was music. Usually a lute was played, while a girl sung poems, often specially written for the occasion. The girls of the family came in to hand around dishes of dainty foods. The dishes were placed on the table and each guest took a little into his bowl for eating. Between courses, fingers were dipped in bowls of scented water, and wiped on silk napkins. The meal was very ceremonious and polite, and even if a festival meal consisted of fifty

B

17

courses, no one could be said to have eaten a great deal. The courses were arranged very carefully so that each one suited the next in flavour and colour. Colour was quite important in a Chinese meal since food was intended to look as palatable as it tasted.

Wine and fruit were served at banquets. There were many kinds of fruit: grapes, pears, melons, mangoes, lichis, and several others. The wines were red and brown, golden and white. But, as with the food, wine was taken only a little at a time, from tiny cups of pottery or silver. Great nobles could drink their wine from cups of white jade, but few ordinary people could afford such luxury.

At the end of a banquet the guests would be entertained with music and dancing by specially-trained troupes of entertainers. All things, from the beginning to the end, came in proper order, so that people got pleasure from things they knew and were not upset by strange surprises. It would have been the height of bad manners to introduce a new kind of food at a feast, or to have the dancers perform a new kind of dance.

The Home

Many millions of Chinese in T'ang times lived in little

Bronze lanterns at the doorway of a rich man's house

huts of mud bricks with a thatched straw roof. Some farming families in the south had bamboo huts with walls of matting. But most people had houses which were more solidly constructed.

Towns were crowded with buildings of all kinds.

There were no special streets of fine houses, but the palaces of rich merchants were built side by side with the little houses of the poor people. The streets were narrow and dirty, with open drains running down the middle. They were always crowded and noisy, but

The garden pavilion of a rich country house

behind the walls of the houses there was peace. A good middle-class house would be built at the back of a small courtyard on the side furthest away from the street. There would be a big hall on the ground floor. At the back of the hall was a special place for the altar, where the tablets of the ancestors were displayed. On either side of this room there might be partitioned-off sleeping places for the elders. A wooden staircase beside a side wall led to an upper storey which was not very high. This was built of painted wood. Here there would be a study, and also the bedrooms for the family. Poor people had to do their cooking in the house, but richer families would have a separate kitchen in the courtyard.

Country houses were much the same as town houses, except that they had room for big gardens around them with ornamental paths. The farmhouses were one-storey buildings with cattle byres and pig pens close to the house so as to save work.

Furniture

T'ang dynasty furniture was quite simple. There were carved wooden tables, high chairs, benches, and stands for holding mirrors, as well as hangers for the little oil lamps and lanterns. Much of the wood was covered by coloured lacquer which was kept gently polished so that it always looked bright and shiny.

There were high tables for people standing up in front of the family altar, and low tables for people writing or eating when sitting on cushions on the floor. But when receiving visitors the family would always sit on chairs, with father looking very important, sitting on a big chair like a throne.

A lady takes tea with her friend

Around the room there were cupboards for keeping the bowls and cups of pottery and silver. Some cupboards held pictures painted on silk rolls, of which one or two were taken to hang on the walls at special times. The Chinese did not like to show many pictures at one time. They preferred to enjoy each one by itself. The paintings were kept rolled up so that they could be taken out of their cupboard whenever they were needed. If a visitor was expected, it was considered good manners to put out a painting specially chosen to please him.

The bedrooms were very simple. The furniture was just a bed and a wardrobe of lacquered wood. Mattresses were hard, stuffed with straw or pads of coarse silk; pillows were blocks of wood or pottery, shaped to fit the curve of the head. Old people sometimes slept on pillows of springy leather. Everybody liked to have a pillow with a poem painted or engraved on it, so that

A pillow made of fine pottery

one should sleep well with pleasant thoughts under the head. The coverlet was made of quilted silk.

Clothes

A gentleman of rank wearing his mandarin's cap

The people of those times liked their clothes to be much softer in shape than modern Chinese costume. Whenever they could afford it, the Chinese wore silk; only the poorer people wore coarse cloth of hemp fibre or of wool. Men and boys wore very baggy trousers held up by a cord like a pyjama cord, and fastened by a cuff at the ankles. Over this came a loose shirt which was worn so as to hang in a fold over the belt. They used this fold instead of pockets. Long jackets without sleeves were sometimes worn, mostly for extra warmth in autumn and winter.

Men of importance wore long gowns made of the richest materials, with long full sleeves, rather like fine dressing-gowns. Around these they bound wide silk sashes. Outdoors they showed their official positions by various kinds of hats which they wore very proudly. Many of them wore turbans made from silk scarves.

Ladies often wore trousers because they were so comfortable. But usually they wore long petticoats and gowns, richly embroidered. The under-gown had a high neck, and the frock was cut with a low neck to show contrasting colours of the gown beneath. A girdle of silk cord or jewelled brocade held the dress in at the waist. Over the dress came a house-coat which was bell skirted, and stiff with embroid-

A lady of fashion
dressed in silk

25

ery. Sleeves were very long, and sometimes quite covered the hands. In fact, dancers had sleeves which ended beyond their hands in a pad of silk which they used to swing in rhythm with their dance.

Chinese women took a great deal of trouble over their toilet. They painted their faces very elegantly, with little rosebud lips, and thin black eyebrows. The face paint was creamy white, with a patch of pink on each cheek, and a blue-green eye shade. How long they took to do their hair is not recorded, but many a princess had poetry read to her while her maids combed and polished her beautiful long black hair. Their mirrors were made of polished white bronze. On the decorated mirror backs there were loops of metal so that they could be hung on a lacquered stand when in use.

Jewellery and Jade

Both men and women wore jewelled ornaments, and fine finger rings of gold and silver. Sometimes for their health they wore rings of copper or even magnetic iron. The rank of an official in the Government was marked by the kind of jewels he wore. But the rank of a lady was less carefully marked. All women of rank loved to wear the most elaborate jewels. They decorated their

26

lovely black hair with diadems and fancy combs of precious metals and jewels, in the form of wings and flowers. Brooches were made like flowers with petals of jewels. Hair-pins of gold had pendants like a rain shower of pearls. Others were made like feathers, glittering with iridescent butterfly wings inlaid in golden

A horse's head carved in jade

wires. They had rings, beads and buttons of many fine stones, if they were rich enough. But most beloved of all stones was jade. It was a magical stone which brought good fortune, and in particular good health, with long life.

Most of the jade came from the mountains of central and southern China. Jade fishers would walk in the cold water of mountain streams feeling the pebbles with their toes. Long practice made them so sensitive that they could feel the difference between stones, and pick out the true jade even if it was covered with a rough, dirty-looking crust like any other stone. They said they could see a kind of steam around the place where jade lay in the water and so knew where to search.

The stone was harder than steel, so it took long hours of work with quartz points and quartz sand to cut through a pebble and polish it. Beads were drilled after weeks of work to make the single hole. Pendants were carved with intricate designs of cloud scrolls, and sacred animals like the dragon and Phoenix, or the long-lived tortoise. So patient was the artist that never a badly-made or roughly-polished piece of jade has come down to us from ancient times. Most precious of all was the creamy "mutton fat" jade, but the mottled rich green jade was not far behind in esteem.

Like most fine things in T'ang China, jade was bought from the shops of tradesmen. It was the most precious thing one could buy.

Shops

While our ancestors were still simple farmers making everything they needed for themselves, the Chinese in the great cities bought everything in shops as we do today, though the shops would seem very strange to us, even in the great capital city of Nanking.

At the back of the shop there was often a wall over

Shops beside a city street

which one could glimpse the green and gold tiles of a
palace. But, however rich the merchant, his shop was
an open-fronted shack. Maybe he had some servants
to bring things out to the customers. Often enough he
would sit on the bench at the far end of the shop and
open his own bundles and boxes of fine things to sell.

29

There were no fixed prices. The merchant would ask twice the value of his goods; the customer would offer half the value. Discussion and friendly talk went on until both sides were satisfied and a price was agreed. The merchant was always ruined by his kindness in selling so cheap, or so he said. The customer always suffered great pain in being forced to pay so much for ordinary things, but that was the correct thing to say. They really felt they had made a good bargain and both sides were pleased.

Factories

Some merchants owned workshops where people worked hard, for long hours, making things for sale. Women would weave and embroider silk. Men would be busy with woodwork and metal work. Many people worked in their own homes, and brought the finished goods to the merchant in the shop. The merchant gave them all the material they needed for the work and paid them a small wage for the time they spent working for him. People were kept very busy in this way. They did not earn much money but, being naturally patient, they were content if they earned enough to keep their family fed and clothed. Most of them lived in the narrow, overcrowded slum quarters of the city. They were proud to own even the roughest small hut of their own. Even the poorest family kept a little altar in one corner of the house for the family prayers. Above it they hung the carved wooden memorial tablets of their ancestors. On festival occasions they brought out their best clothes from camphor-wood chests, and looked as rich as their neighbours. The Chinese were a proud people and loved to appear well among their equals. There was always respect for human beings of all kinds. Even the poorest beggars who could not work were looked after. It was said the beggar might have a son who would pass his examinations and become Prime Minister to the Emperor. Then the beggar would be lifted up by his son and made a great man. Maybe he would reward those who had been kind to him.

The Potters

Among the busiest of all workpeople in T'ang China were the potters. They lived in villages of their own, near places where good clay could be dug. A few of them would leave the village to keep shops in the big towns. Their clay was carried in to them from the

T'ang tomb figures, a camel and a groom

village, and their shops were used by all the village potters as a place to sell their wares.

Potters were usually peasant farmers as well, growing food for their families. They could not spare much time for potting in seasons of sowing and harvest. They dug the clay after the rains had softened it. They preferred to fire their pots in the kilns when the harvest was over and there was plenty of dry straw and bamboo to eke out the scarce wood to keep the fires going. They planned their work very exactly, and they even watched the direction of the winds to make quite sure there would be a good draught to help the firing of the kilns.

People treated potters with great respect in China. They were the most important of all the craftsmen. At one period they even refused to make a set of special vases for an Emperor because the weather had been bad and many of them were ill. The Emperor preferred to wait for his beautiful vases rather than spoil the temper of the potters.

Making a T'ang Horse

The most famous of all T'ang works of art are the pottery horses which were buried in the tombs of great men. They came into fashion when the second T'ang Emperor, Tai Tsung, decreed that his tomb must be decorated with images of the eight fine chargers who accompanied him into battle and more than once had saved his life. When the Emperor had horses made for his burial, all the lesser officials of his court found that horses were necessary for their comfort in the other world. Most officials went further than ordinary people in preparing for death. Everyone had a place for a grave, and his coffin was made as soon as he had a house of his own. But the officials prepared the furnishing of their tombs in advance. However, most of them could not face the danger of having fragile pottery figures about the house where they might so easily be broken before they were used. So the potters were always prepared to make pottery horses quickly, when they heard of the death of some important man.

In the workshops the potters had a number of baked clay moulds of parts of horses. There were heads,

One of the memorial carvings from the tomb of Tai Tsung

Painted wood model of a horse to be copied in clay

bodies, tails, necks, straight legs, bent legs, and charging legs. They had been made from carved wooden figures, and were cut deep to give good sharp lines on the moulded copies. The craftsman chose his set of piece moulds for the horse he was going to make. Then he rolled out pieces of white clay mixed with crushed fire-clay, as if he were making pastry. The strips of clay were laid in the moulds and pressed firmly into the shape. When the clay dried, it shrank and so came loose

35

from the moulds. The pieces were then joined together by wetting the edges to soften the clay a little, and then pressing them firmly together. It was possible to assemble two horses made from the same set of moulds in such a way that they looked quite different. Thick clay at the joints between the pieces allowed one to give the neck a different angle, or to set the head with a different twist. The legs, too, could be set in slightly different positions. When the horse was all together, it was put in a cool place to dry steadily for some hours.

If it was going to be a specially good horse, the boys in the potter's workshop would paint it over quickly with a thin coat of powdered kaolin (china clay) which dried quickly and left the model horse with a brilliant white surface.

The best horses were glazed; that is, they were painted with a mixture of a little clay and crushed galena, a kind of lead ore. This dried very quickly. Next, the boys came round and splashed the horse with paint brushes dipped in a thick paint made of green copper carbonate from the mountains of Turkestan, or brown ochres from local rocks, and even iron rust. The whole horse was then put in a fire-clay box near the kiln to dry thoroughly in the warmth. The kiln was a small arched room of fire-bricks. At the bottom was space for fire-wood to be packed in; half-way up, there were shelves for supporting the boxes, or saggars, holding the horses, and at the far side was a chimney for taking the smoke away.

The warm kiln was closed down when all the boxes were in. Bundles of firewood and straw were packed in underneath and lit. The flames roared round the fire-clay boxes with the horses inside. They became hotter and hotter. At about 500° Centigrade the clay was completely hardened, and, as the horses turned red hot, the glaze began to melt. The splashes of mineral paint ran into it. At about 950° Centigrade the firing was finished. It sometimes took a whole night of watching the fire and keeping it stoked with firewood before the potter saw the saggars glowing with the right pinky-golden colour which told him the work was done. Then very gradually the fire was allowed to die down, and the kiln cooled. In half a day it was cooled enough to be opened and the boxes removed. Very gently they were opened and inside each of them stood a pottery horse with a shiny new glaze covering it. The green dots had become splashes of a much deeper green, and the ochre and iron rust had become areas of golden brown glaze.

In this way a set of horses for a funeral could be made in less than three days. If the potters had followed their usual practice and fired their pot before glazing, and then fired again to glaze the pot, another day would

37

have been lost and the ceremonies for the official funeral put all out of order.

As well as horses, the T'ang potters made figures of the guardian spirits of the underworld, and delightful little figures of men and women intended to symbolise the pleasures of life in the next world. From them we

T'ang pottery figures of a
dancing girl and a lady of the Court

learn a great deal of how the Chinese in those long ago days dressed and danced. Sometimes the figures were glazed, but in many cases they were painted in matt colours after they had come out of the kiln, which made them appear still more life-like than if they were glazed.

Trade

In T'ang times China was so rich and powerful that people seemed more alive than usual. They were always experimenting to find newer and better ways of doing things.

Potters found many new ways of treating their clay. Workers in metal, leather and wood found new designs were coming to them through the contact with India and Persia in trade. Great caravans of traders came buying and selling from all the surrounding countries. The Chinese passed over their fine roads and into other countries. Ponies and donkeys carried goods in big basketry panniers, over long journeys. In the mountains of Tibet the loads were sometimes divided into much smaller packs, to be carried by trains of yaks taking treasures of silk and pottery to the markets of India. Far to the west the roads led into the deserts, where the two-humped Bactrian camels took their loads to carry

39

Loading yaks for a caravan trading through Tibet

across the shifting sands. Wonderful things were taken
to the capital of the Caliphs of Baghdad; and the
Chinese traders even found their way to the great markets of Constantinople. Everywhere they went they
took silk and fine pottery.

The Borders of China

Travellers coming to trade in China from the west found
their way was carefully guarded. As they came to the

frontier posts, they would find horsemen armed with swords and short, powerful bows of springy horn. They would ride up to the caravans and escort them to their guard-room. Nobody would risk trying to fight these keen-eyed warriors if they wished to enter the Silk Land, as they called it. In the guard-house the leaders of the caravan would be questioned. Had they come as peaceful traders, or teachers of some new religion, or to bring gifts to the Emperor? Which towns did they intend to visit? How long would they stay? When the questions were all answered, they would be given an escort of soldiers to guard them to the nearest town. The leader of the escort carried a tablet of wood painted with Chinese signs. When he reached town he would give this to the Captain of the town guard so that he should know the strangers had been examined at the frontier.

The Defences

As the caravan advanced towards China they would approach their first cities. Sometimes on the way they would notice a cloud of dust on the horizon. The soldiers would tell them it might be a raiding party of Mongols or even of Tartars. But it was not often that open attacks were made on well-defended caravans. If a raiding party was bold enough to attack, it was usually from an ambush in some dried-up stream bed in the desert, or from behind the shelter of sand dunes.

The raiders would rush out of cover and try to cut off the last few carts and baggage animals from the convoy. As they charged, they might try to scare the merchants by shooting off some whistling arrows which screamed overhead as the real, sharp, bronze-tipped arrows began to fall. But usually the soldiers of the rear-guard would

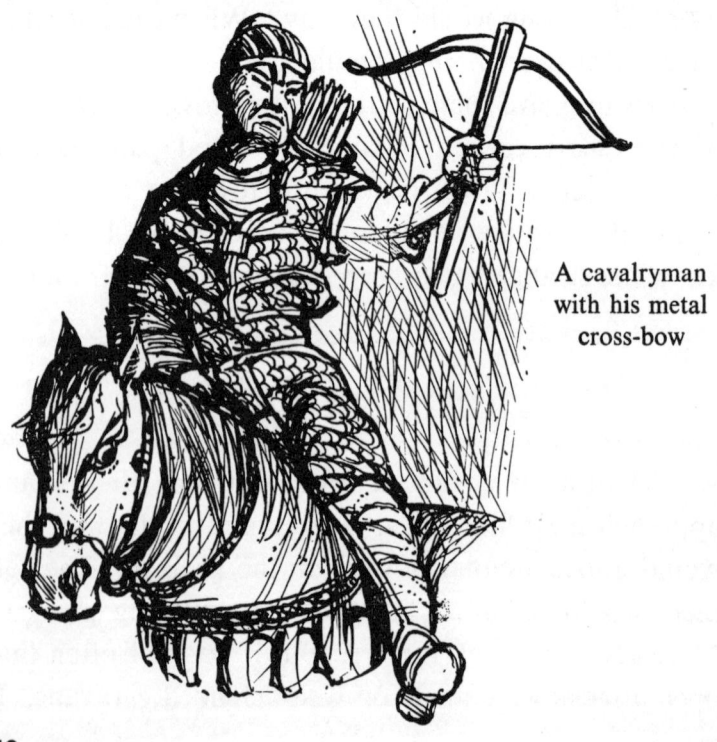

A cavalryman with his metal cross-bow

fan out on their strong little horses to protect the caravan. They wore armour of thick padded silk, covered
with plates of hard leather, or sometimes of steel. Their
horses wore rather similar armour and, though sturdy
and strong, they could not be so fast as the horses of
the raiding tribesmen who carried no armour. However,
the Chinese warriors would space themselves in a semi-
circle and whip out their horn bows so as to put up a
barrage of arrows. A good archer was able to shoot so
rapidly that, when his first arrow was striking the target,
another was flying through the air and the third was just
leaving his bow. The target was usually one of the
raiders' horses.

The Chinese army horses were trained to charge, and
also to stand still, in spite of danger. They gave their
riders a steady seat from which to shoot their arrows.
So, even if the raiders tried their trick of pretending to
ride away and suddenly turn to shoot backwards, there
was a good chance that the arrows of the soldiers would
reach them first and kill them. The army was trained as
much for steadiness in defence as for bravery in attack.
They knew very well that, if the enemy spent all their
energy in wild charges which were beaten off time after
time, they would finally gallop away and not return.

Only if there was a threat from a really big and well-
organised army would the Chinese soldiers form up to

attack. They would then charge with short strong lances levelled at the enemies. The archers fired a cloud of arrows from behind. On the wings, lighter horsemen whirled into the attack. Sometimes they had a force of warriors who would charge across the front of the enemy in chariots. As they passed, they shot heavy arrows and threw javelins to break up the line and make it easier for the horsemen to break through in their charge.

When the slow charge of the heavily-armed horsemen struck the enemy force, little resistance was possible. Even if horsemen were dismounted when their horses were speared, they were well protected by their quilted armour, and were able to struggle up again. They would then go to help their comrades by clearing a path with their heavy chopping swords. The aim was always to capture the general of the enemy forces, or to make him run away in disgrace.

In such battles the Emperor Tai Tsung often fought personally on one or other of his eight great horses. He was a wise and great general who was never defeated.

Frontier Cities

On approaching a city outside the frontiers of China, one saw little else but a great wall of brick or stone. It

The Great Wall of China

was four times the height of a man, and sloped a little inwards. Along the top was a broad pathway with walls in which one noticed the threatening arrow slits. A few great gateways broke the grim wall. These were single arches through which the road passed. They could be closed by giant wooden doorways covered with bronze studs and plates. Above them, on the top of the wall, were guard towers, squat massive buildings with low roofs of thick pottery tiles. It was almost impossible to set such towers on fire by shooting flaming arrows on them. There were spouts in these towers for pouring down boiling oil and burning pitch on any enemy who was foolish enough to come close under them. Such gateways in the city walls were very strong fortresses indeed.

However, when traders and travellers came in peace, the great gates were open, and the fortress guards were ready to welcome their fellow soldiers who were escorting the caravan. Within the gates they entered a busy Chinese city, which was not only a frontier fortress, but also a place where traders could rest and do business with local Chinese merchants.

Before travellers were allowed to go to a rest house, they were taken before the City Governor who was always a Mandarin of high rank. They entered the palace with their servants, bearing presents for the great man. As the representative of the Emperor, he had to be treated with great respect. His visitors were expected to kow-tow before him; that is, they would kneel before him and then bow down until their foreheads touched the floor. This was done either three or nine times, according to the importance of the Governor. After the merchants had told of their business, and laid their

Merchants before a
City Governor

presents wrapped in silk scarves before the Mandarin,
they awaited his orders. If all was well, they were told
where they could find a place to stay in the city, and
were given a tablet with a safe conduct to the next city.
They bowed as they walked backwards through the hall.
As they passed the silken curtains of the door, they
turned to find other parcels of goods, which they pre-
sented to the soldiers of their escort. Thus all was made

47

friendly in a polite way without any fuss or asking for presents.

In the city they found sellers of sweetmeats and cooked food, so that a quick meal was possible at any time. Many shops displayed painted boards which told of the treasures within. From the tea houses there came music and singing. They glimpsed the slow posturing of the gorgeously dressed dancing girls, and heard the

Visitors arriving at a Chinese tea house

polite murmur of applause from the audience of tea-drinkers. They would move on, seeking their rest house. Here they found a big courtyard surrounded with stables for horses and camels, and rooms with strong doors for protecting their stores of merchandise. At one end was the house, with its big hall and many small bedrooms. In fact, such a caravanserai was almost like a well-organised modern hotel. In such a city, foreign traders would first come to understand the Chinese way of life. They rapidly learned that the Chinese were very friendly people indeed, but that they were not interested in the ways of their guests. Every Chinaman was quite sure that the Chinese way of life was the best, and that foreigners were friendly, but badly-educated, barbarians.

After a few days, the caravan of traders would move on with its loads of valuables. The Chinese welcomed gold from India, furs from the West and minerals from Persia to make fine glazes on their pottery. Muslins and ivory from India were brought to market, together with still more valuable books from the centres of the Buddhist religion. In the caravans there were often Buddhist monks coming to teach their religion, or Nestorian Christians from Syria also seeking to convert the great country of the Rising Sun to their own beliefs. T'ang China welcomed them all in friendship, so

D

long as they did not interfere with the rule of the Emperor.

Once the caravan had passed through the gateways in the already ancient Great Wall of China, they seemed to be in a new world. Instead of the occasional oasis, and the plantations in the few river beds near the desert roads, they came into a land where every square yard of earth was used. Little farms, with one-storey farmhouses and a chequer of tiny fields around them, seemed everywhere. Villages clustered round crossroads and beside the rivers. Even the apparently wild

The great gateway in a city wall

woodlands in the mountains were in reality carefully planted and trees were regularly cut as they reached their full growth. Each section of woodland belonged to some village. No land was wasted.

Roads

In T'ang China there were as many and as good roads as there were in the Roman Empire. However, the Chinese roads only ran straight when passing over flat country. Even then they would occasionally bend around some piece of especially valuable farm land. In the mountains the roads always took the easiest way up the winding valleys. In some cases they were diverted so that travellers could enjoy some particularly wonderful view. The Chinese were not so interested as the Romans in getting from one place to another by the shortest possible route. Instead of the straight roads for marching armies, they built easy roads for trading caravans with animals and carts. Near a great city the roads were often taken a little further round so as to pass through beautiful scenery and make the city appear more attractive when it was first seen by the traveller.

Between farms and villages there were lesser roads. Some were just well-trodden footpaths, where people usually carried loads from one place to another on their backs. Sometimes a horseman on official business would gallop over them, but in winter they were so muddy that foot travel was easier. Other local roads were lined with a paved track down the middle to take the single wheel of the enormous wheelbarrows which farmers used to take their produce to market. Bullock

A country farmer's bullock cart

carts with very broad wheels could move over the softer side tracks of such a road. The smaller roads went round farms, and wandered from village to village. The peasant farmers had used them for centuries when working, and they preferred to go a long way round rather than take a short cut across another farmer's land. These were not roads for hurried travellers.

The Capital City

As the main roads came down to the wide plains of the lowlands, travellers passed through a country of swampy rice fields, and little rocky hills thrusting up from under the deep alluvial soil. Lakes abounded, and the slow streams were filled with water lilies and fish. The great river and the canals were thronged with barges, and at last the traveller would

A T'ang period pagoda

see in the distance the city now called Nanking, which then was the capital of China. Outside the city were numberless villages on either side of the great river Yangtze Kiang which ran beside the walls. On the hills were stone pagodas, and beautifully-decorated memorial gateways. On specially chosen slopes one passed the carefully-kept graveyards. This was a world in which religion and nature seemed to be combined quite naturally.

Over the smaller rivers there were high arched bridges. They were often steep to climb up, but very beautiful to look at. On the great river Yangtze there were multitudes of barges and houseboats. Here and there by the quays were great three-masted trading junks which had brought jewels and camphor, as well as the precious swallows' nests for making soup, all from the islands of Indonesia. What a fine city this was, with river and roads leading to the gateways in its massive walls! Even the outer city wall was decorated with fine carvings; and great stone lions and dragons were set up near the

Ships at a quayside on the Yangtze

gateways. The tiles on the roofs of the guard-houses were all glazed in golden yellow and jade green. The city gates were covered with bronze, and coloured lacquers. The stone-paved highways led through them, past the bravely – armoured guards, into the great city where at least two million people lived.

A palanquin used by ladies for travelling in town

At first the T'ang capital looked like any other Chinese city. The main roads were broad and well paved, but they ran through a maze of narrow alleyways with the usual open drains running down the centre. The people were well dressed, except for the beggars, whose rags were almost a uniform intended to excite pity. But in some ways the people seemed to be more busy with serious things; there were more soldiers in finer uniforms, more important people in their sedan chairs travelling from one part to another. It was indeed a rich Capital city of a great empire.

Within the city was another city surrounded by a fine wall of its own. Here was a town of lovely palaces and pagodas set in parks amidst trees. The great officials of the state had their palaces, and the principal offices of the Civil Service were housed here. Among the most important groups of buildings were the Examination Halls, which were open to all who wished to enter the service of the Emperor. Any Chinese boy could come here to sit at one of the great annual examinations. All had a fair chance and it might well be that the Emperor himself would visit the halls to see that all was being conducted fairly. Yet even within this city of beautiful parks and buildings there was still another wall and another small city of wonder in which dwelt the Emperor, with his officials and wives and servants. Here also were the sacred places, where the Emperor made offerings to the Heavenly Power for his people.

The Emperor

Most people never saw the Emperor. Tai Tsung was quite exceptional because he led his armies personally. He also travelled about the country making sure that his people were wisely governed by his ministers. Many great cities in China had seen this short, thick-set man, in armour of silk and gold, ride through the streets on his beautiful chestnut charger. He liked to feed his horses himself, and was very proud of them. The people admired him because he was a friendly man who shared their love of horses, and because he was a brave soldier.

The Emperor was believed to be a member of a family chosen to rule by the Heavenly Power, to whom he made offerings on behalf of all his people each New Year. Because of his position, the Emperor was believed to unite the powers of Heaven and Earth, and was compelled to rule over China for the good of his people. Not all the Emperors were such great men as Tai Tsung. Many of them became cruel and oppressive, but the people believed that this was a natural event. They thought that it was the law of Heaven that everything should begin well, and grow, and then become weak and pass away. This state of change affected families of Emperors just as much as it did the plants in the fields. So when an Emperor was a bad man it was felt perfectly right to throw him out.

It must have been very difficult indeed to be a good emperor. He was treated almost like a god. His wonderful palace of scented woods and gold was in the midst

The Emperor in his home

of a beautiful park. He was served on plates of gold and silver. Even his greatest ministers were expected to crawl on hands and knees before him and bang their heads on the floor at his feet. It was only too easy for him to forget his duties and spend his time seeking pleasures for himself. Only a truly great man could stand all this inhuman glory without becoming mad.

58

In public life the Emperor was the centre of all power. He appointed the great officials who were to serve him. He personally chose the generals who were to lead his armies. The Ministers who looked after trade, finance, and industries, and the Viceroys who governed the provinces in the name of the Emperor, were entirely dependent upon his good will for their position and their life. In turn, they appointed officers of lesser rank who were obedient to the written laws of the country. Thus the Emperor was able to keep control of affairs without knowing every detail of administration.

The Examinations

The T'ang Emperors brought back into use an ancient system of examinations by which they selected officials for their Civil Service. The system was based on the ancient books which we call the Chinese Classics. These were books about how people should treat one another, written by great wise men of the past. They were rather like some of the books of the Old Testament in the Bible, and not at all like the Greek or Roman classics.

Any youngster who wished to become an official in government service under the T'ang Emperors had to take an examination in his knowledge of these sacred

The great hall of examinations

books. It was thought that if he had worked hard to fit himself for the examination, and had the energy to travel to the examination halls, he deserved a chance to sit for the test. Thus all who chose to come were welcome to try for a pass. It was believed that, if a boy could show a good knowledge of the classics, he must have strength of character and was less likely to be tempted to act unjustly for his own profit when he became an

A carved wooden foot rule

official. He could learn the details of his work when he was doing it, but he could not learn to be a wise and good man unless he really understood the teachings contained in the sacred books.

At the time when the thunderstorms marked the beginning of the year, young men from all parts of the Empire came to the capital for examination. Each was allotted a place to sit in the Examination Halls, and given a numbered ticket. He brought his own writing set of brushes, and a stick of hard black ink, with the grinding palette, which he used to grind his ink with water. All the candidates were searched to make sure they had brought no hidden notes with them. Then each one was given his sheets of paper, stamped with the number of his place and the name of the examiner.

The examiner read out a short passage from one of the classics. The boys took their brushes and wrote it down. Then they had to compose an essay which

Chinese writing

61

explained the meaning of the passage. Usually the examination lasted three days and the candidates had to write a series of such essays.

The whole examination was fair. A candidate found cheating was thrown out and never permitted to sit for another official examination. If an examiner was found to have been unfair, he was publicly disgraced by being paraded around the streets with a notice round his neck telling of his crime. Then his head was cut off. Fairness was very important because the task of the examiner was to select the very best candidates for official posts. If a young man was successful at this examination, he might continue to rise from one position to another until he became governor of a great province.

As soon as a young man had passed the examination, work was found for him. He was usually sent to some part of the Empire far away from his home province. If he was clever and honest, promotions awaited him. But personal character always counted a great deal in China. A good man who showed mercy in his judgments was preferred to any tyrant.

The Tradesmen

Most Chinese did not want to become officials, or to

join the army. However great these careers might make them, they preferred to stay in the family business. Sometimes these family businesses had been running for centuries. There were carvers of jade and hard stone, woodworkers, metal smiths, potters, leather workers, silk weavers and people in hundreds of other trades. Even the families who spent their lives sorting out the usable things from the garbage heaps of the cities felt that they were members of an honourable profession, and as worthy of respect as the bankers and fortune-tellers. They even had their own particular patron god, with a special temple where they met occasionally to make offerings and ask for help in their trade. There was no Sabbath day of rest in ancient China. Life just went on and on, and people went to the temples when-ever they wished. However, as the seasons of the year and the phases of the moon, as well as many other special days, were marked by gay holiday festivals, no one overworked.

Theatres and Plays

People did not take much time for recreation. However, they delighted in going to the theatre, and were quite capable of sitting through a play lasting for three days.

The Chinese theatre had its famous writers, and they preferred a kind of historical pageant play as their theme. Excitement and romance kept the audience eagerly watching the bare stage. There was much music, and sometimes the action of the play was so formal as to appear like a rather stately ballet. The actors wore fantastic and beautiful costumes, but there was no scenery. A painted board was carried in between acts to tell the

An actor dancing the part
of an archer in battle

audience where the scene was supposed to take place. There were no actresses. Women made the costumes, and dressed the actors, but on the stage no woman would appear. As in Shakespeare's time in England, all the ladies' parts were acted by boys.

The music was composed to make the audience happy or sad, in accordance with the mood of the play, as they sat and watched. From time to time they would open their little bundles of food and eat a light meal as the

The Court Poet
recites sonnets
for a play

E

play went on. If the play was a very famous one, most people would know it by heart, and they would prompt the actors by reciting lines for them if they forgot. Whether the play was given in a great hall of some nobleman or in a simple tent of poles and matting, the audience would be just as interested and would live the parts of the performers as if they were themselves on the stage.

Since most people could neither read nor write, the theatre was a means by which they could live in history, and learn literature by hearing it. They loved to recite poetry. In Chinese the spoken words are sung in various tones so that a poem recited could sound like strange music. Most of the T'ang-period poems were quite short verses about the beauty of flowers and the pleasures of family life. The most famous of their poets was Li Tai Po, a very shy man who was often only persuaded to write a poem when his friends made him drunk.

Music

To many people Chinese music sounds very strange. That is because the scale used is only to be found in China. It is based on natural sounds like the tinkle of dripping water, the cries of birds and the crash of

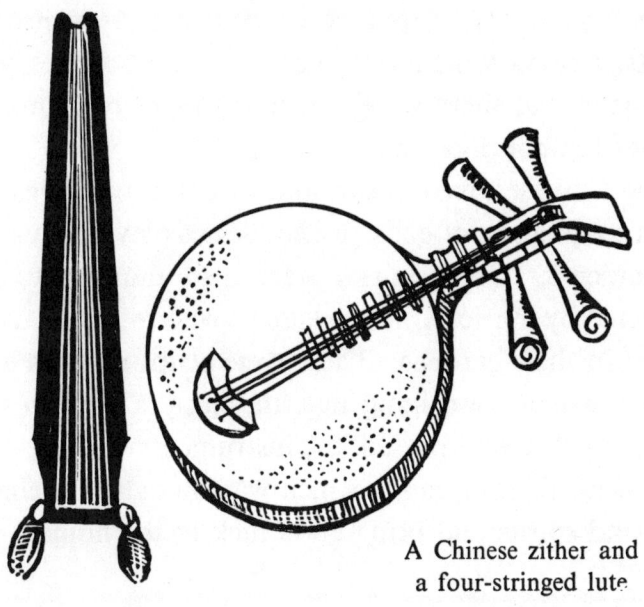

A Chinese zither and
a four-stringed lute

thunder. There was no written music, but musicians learned directly from one another. The names of the notes they played helped them to keep the music in their minds. A wrong note would not only sound out of place, but it would have a wrong name which would not fit into the pattern of words of the composition.

Although the theory of music was so different from that of European peoples, the instruments were rather similar. There was a family of stringed instruments, including mandolines, lutes and zithers. The wind instruments were mostly flutes and whistles, with some

oboes and horns. Percussion included strange instruments, among which were gongs of hard stones and
even jade, but there were also many types of drum, as
well as tambourines and cymbals.

The Chinese loved music, and in T'ang paintings we
often see pictures of gods and goddesses playing musical
instruments. Good fairies were also thought to be
attracted by music. Chinese ladies loved to have "wind
bells" in their gardens. These were strips of glass and
bronze which were hung in little clusters high in the
trees. As the wind passed, the instruments would make
a pleasant tinkling music which was thought to delight
the wind spirits and bring good luck to the home.

Silk

Women were the chief makers of silk goods in T'ang
times. The art was regarded as a secret to be kept from
the knowledge of foreigners. Although great quantities
of this lovely material were taken in trade to Rome and
Constantinople, no one in the West knew the secret of
its manufacture. Travellers were carefully kept away
from the silk farms. The Emperor knew very well that
a great part of his wealth came from the silk trade
through Asia to Europe.

Silk was made from the cocoons of the silk moth. The moth laid its eggs on the mulberry leaves of the farm. Later they hatched out as little "silk-worms", which set to work busily eating the leaves of the mulberry trees. No other food would satisfy them. As they were kept indoors, the children were constantly picking fresh leaves to feed them. After a few months the little caterpillars started to change. They threw out thin strands

Girls winding threads of raw silk

of silk, finer than a spider's web, and wrapped themselves up in it until they became little cream-coloured bundles about the size of a plum stone. Some of these cocoons were kept for breeding new silk moths. But most of them were collected before the new moth could form and eat its way out of its ball of silk. They were gently turned until a free end of the silk was found, and then dropped in boiling hot water. Very slowly the silk was unwound by hand. You can imagine how delicate this was if you think of undoing a spider's web without breaking the thread! As it came free, it was wound on a big wheel made of a frame holding silk threads on which the new silk rested. When sufficient silk had been run on to the frame, it was put aside to wait until other frames had been filled. Three or four frames were then hung up side by side, and slowly turned. As they rotated, strands of silk, one from each frame, were twisted together to form a thread.

Dyeing

The silk thread was reeled in its turn, and made up into large hanks of thread ready for dyeing. Most families could prepare simple dyes from madder which gave a red-brown colour, and from indigo for blue. But for anything special, the silk was taken to a proper dyer's workshop where it was soaked and dipped in colour solutions and often boiled in them. So, when they came to make cloth from the thread, the weavers had a great range of colours to choose from, much more than could be produced by the silk farmers themselves.

The dyers knew many intricate ways of dyeing thread in patterns. In some cases the threads were stretched on a loom ready to be used as the warp in weaving. Next, they were tied tightly in selected spots, so that the ties made a pattern. Then the whole frame was dipped in dye. The parts which were tied up would not take the colour. So when the cloth was taken out of the dye, washed, and the ties removed, a white pattern was left on the coloured warp. When the cloth was woven, this pattern came out as a light-coloured speckled design on the finished cloth. There were a few amazingly clever weavers who could dye the weft threads (the ones which run across the cloth) in the same way, so that when woven, the warp and weft came together to make a clear white pattern on the coloured background.

Excavations in the ruined cities of the old silk road across Turkestan have shown us that the T'ang dyers knew all about batik dyeing in silk. They took a white piece of silk, coated parts of it with fine wax, or perhaps a thick rice paste. Then they dipped it into a bath of dye. When it was taken out it was put into hot water and the paste washed out. The parts which had been "reserved" by the paste were left white. One could do this many times with one piece of cloth, "reserving" different parts, and mixing colours. It took a great amount of patience but the result was very attractive, especially on a piece of soft shiny silk.

Weaving

The weavers of T'ang China knew all that there was to know about weaving without machine power. Their looms were upright frames around which the warp threads were laid. There was a simple arrangement of threads put around alternate warps so that they could be pulled out for the shuttle to pass between them. However, these "heddles" were arranged so that they pulled up warps in a pattern. It was possible either to weave plain cloth, or actually weave a rich brocade pattern into the cloth as one went along. The heddles were worked by pedals, so that the weaver, perched on a cross bar which served as a seat, could use both arms freely to throw the shuttle holding the weft thread through the cloth. In this way cloth could be made up to five feet wide.

Weaving silk curtains on a brocade loom

Some districts specialised in their own kinds of cloth. Some families, too, wove complicated brocades on special looms by their own carpenters. Nearly all Chinese industry in those days was in the hands of families of specialists. They would never allow people who were not members of the family to learn their secrets. However, they occasionally allowed young people who married into the family to take part in their trade. As

73

they depended on selling the things which they made, their work was always carefully done. It was part of the good name of a family that they never turned out bad work.

Woodwork

Chinese woodworking tools were of excellent design, even compared with our own today. They used saws and chisels, and their hand drills were used with fixed bits. Draw knives and scrapers were used more than planes, but they had many kinds of specially-shaped planes for making decorative mouldings on their furniture.

They did a great deal of skilled wood carving, using mallets and chisels exactly as we do. Joints were fitted very exactly. In fact, carpenters could make water pumps of wood which could lift water from a stream without leaking at all. When making furniture they preferred to fit everything together so exactly that it would be held tightly in place by a few wedges, or by wooden dowels fitted into holes bored to take them. They avoided using nails because they felt that a good woodworker should use all wood. Even when building the elaborate wooden framework of a palace, they fitted it all together precisely, treating a beam thicker-than a man with the same delicate exactness with which they would make a little box for holding writing brushes.

〜〜〜〜〜〜〜〜〜〜〜〜〜〜〜〜〜〜〜〜〜〜〜

Lacquer

〜〜〜〜〜〜〜〜〜〜〜〜〜〜〜〜〜〜〜〜〜

In T'ang times lacquer work was very popular in China.

A coloured lacquer dish

Quite small articles were decorated with lacquer, and great walls were similarly prepared. Lacquer preserved wood by giving it a hard shiny surface, which did not easily wear away. It could be made very beautiful with its colours of red, yellow, brown and black.

Lacquer was prepared from the oily sap of a tree. This was collected by cutting grooves in the bark to lead the sap into little spouts which dripped into pottery containers. As soon as a container was full, it was covered and sealed down. That was important because the liquid began to harden as soon as it came into contact with the oxygen in the air. Once a skin had formed, it had to be taken out and thrown away before the rest of the lacquer could be used.

The lacquer was mixed with colour before use. Fine lamp black, or yellow ochre, or mercuric oxide were used to give black, yellow and red. They were powdered as finely as could be, and then stirred rapidly into the jars of lacquer which were quickly covered up again.

When in use, the lacquer was brushed quickly and smoothly over the wood. The aim of the workman was to make the layer as thin as possible. As soon as the work was painted, it was put into a damp place to dry very slowly, so that the lacquer would become very hard. When it was dry, another coat was applied in the same way. It might well be that forty or fifty very thin coats of lacquer were put on a box before it was considered fit for final preparation. Sometimes coats of different colour were put on, so that when the surface was ornamented with carving, the different colours would show through. Sometimes the lacquer was cut right through into the wood by sharp steel knives so that beautiful pearl-shell inlay work could be set in the lacquer.

Pottery

When lacquer work was in use, it could easily be kept

polished by a servant girl wiping it over with a piece of silk. Maybe it was because lacquer could be kept so beautifully clean and shiny that Chinese potters tried out so many wonderful glazes for their pots.

A white
T'ang vase

As we know, pottery was made by whole villages of potters. In each district the kind of pottery was different because of the difference in the clays which could be found locally. But everywhere in T'ang times they were trying to find ways of firing the clay at higher and higher temperatures. In districts where China clay (kaolin) and China stone (petuntse) could be found, there were the beginnings of beautiful porcelain. This can only be made when the clay is so hot that it begins to melt within a mould in the kiln.

Potters were very careful to mix their clay well by kneading it like dough on a block of stone. When it was quite smooth and even all through, the wet clay was given to the thrower. He took a handful big enough to make the pot he wanted to throw. This was slapped down on the middle of the potter's wheel. The wheel was nearly a yard across, and some six inches thick. It was pivoted very exactly on a cone of iron or stone set in the ground. Usually the wheel was of heavy wood,

77

The potter beginning to shape a vase

but some potters used old mill stones. Once the ball of
clay was in the middle of the wheel, the potter stuck a
wooden handle in a hole near the edge of the wheel, and
used it to spin the wheel round and round. Gradually he
made it spin faster and faster. At the right speed he
whipped out the handle, and squatted down beside his
wheel. He dipped his hands in water, joined them and,
stretching out his bare arms, he pushed his thumbs into
the middle of the ball of clay. Then with fingers and

78

thumb he delicately drew up the clay while the wheel was spinning. Small cups and bowls could be finished on one spinning of the wheel before it slowed down too much. But when the potter was making large vases, he had to stop and then spin the wheel to full speed two or three times before the pot was shaped. Once the shape was right, the pot was cut off the wheel by a piece of wire pulled under it. Then it was very gently lifted off the wheel and put on a board to dry in a shady corner of the workshop.

Some potters fired their pots in a kiln at this stage. When these came out of the kiln, they were hard and white, ready to be painted with specially-mixed glazes made of china clay, and various colours made from powdered minerals. Other potters preferred to paint the unfired pot with a coat of china clay and relied on drying it carefully before glazing it in one burning in the village kilns.

The village kilns were a string of arched brick chambers, each with a little doorway in the side. They usually ran up a hillside, like a great serpent. Each chamber had shelves round the sides. Here the boys who slipped in through the door at the side arranged the pots in fire-clay boxes without lids. Thus the pots were protected from direct contact with burning wood which would either crack them or blacken them.

Part of a kiln,
drawn to show the pots inside

Each chamber was joined to the next by an archway at front and back. This ensured that the fire should rush through from one kiln chamber to another up the slope of the hill. At the sides were removable bricks, so that new wood could be pushed into the kiln during firing.

Most pottery-firing took place in the autumn. Work on the fields was over. Firewood, bamboo, and grass had been collected. The position of the moon was right, and the astrologers had said which was the lucky night. The kiln was packed. Each family filled its own section of the great fire-brick tunnel. Then the little doorways were bricked up. The village leader threw a flaming torch into the piles of grass and wood in the bottom kiln. The flame caught, and soon smoke began to come out of the top end of the kiln up the hill. Every now and then the potters would peep into their part of the kiln to see that all was well. As they closed the little peep-holes, they would signal to the boys of the family to open a brick at the side and push in more wood. Gradually the long kiln began to look like a fiery dragon, spitting out flame and sparks. Red glowing patches showed when the fire bricks were taken out in order to add wood. Sparks would burst out every time this was done. It was a lovely sight, and the potters made it a village festival. They sat up all night working at the kilns and eating and drinking happily at every spare minute.

Most of the pots would be white or cream in colour, some a little more brownish. We should call them stone ware. Some of the whiter ones were almost porcelain. But in the time of Tai Tsung the potters had not discovered how to make a true porcelain.

Some days later the potters would wreathe their pots with ropes of straw to protect them, and carry enormous loads of them on their backs, or on the giant wheelbarrows of China, down to the market town. They did not earn a great deal of money, but they always hoped that one day a visitor from the Imperial Court would command them to make a special pot.

F

Lamps and Lighting

Among their other wares the potters made little crusie lamps. These lamps burnt oil. A wick at one end burnt with a clear white light from either almond oil or cabbage-seed oil. Big houses had lamp stands with several stages of little lamps built into them. When lit up, they must have looked like little trees with leaves of light. But very poor people might have to make do with lamps made out of shells, or even smoky torches.

The Chinese were no strangers to candles made of wax and mutton fat. They made them of many sizes, from tiny ones as big as your little finger, to great ones bigger than a man's arm, which were used in temples. They also made candles of wax mixed with scented powdered wood, which burnt very slowly and steadily. They marked these candles with names of hours, so that they recorded the time as they burnt. Although not quite exact, they were very useful to people who had to work at night.

In the cities a few streets were lit at night with torches and lanterns. When travelling at night, most people liked to carry lanterns with them. They lit up the road, rather faintly, but they also kept off the darkness demons. This was important in ancient China because

people were very super-
stitious and felt afraid
at night.

Horn lanterns were
made in great numbers.
They were prepared from
the horns of the water
buffalo which patiently
drew the ploughs and
heavy carts in the coun-
try farms. Horns were
cleaned carefully, and
then put in a pan of
hot salty water. The
water softened the horn
and allowed the lantern-

A girl travelling with a
lantern at night

makers to split off the layers one at a time. These sheets
of horn were clear and a pale creamy colour. If the water
had boiled, they would have been spoilt and become opa-
que. While they were still wet and soft, the horn layers
were put in a wooden press. As they flattened under the
pressure, they slowly dried and hardened again. After the
flattened pieces of horn had been cut into shape, they
were fitted into lanterns usually made of strips of cane.
The bottom, where the candle was fixed, could be un-
clipped and taken out of the lantern. The lantern itself

was usually carried on a cane or a crooked stick. One could hold it out to light up things in front, or lower it to see if the ground were safe to walk on.

Festival Processions

On great occasions the Chinese liked to crowd out into streets for celebrations. They had many festivals: for

Crowds gathering for the

the New Moons, the Spring Flowers, Midsummer, the Autumn, the Winter Solstice, and festivals of the local gods. These were happy days and nights when everyone crowded into the streets to celebrate. At night they carried lanterns, from temple to temple. In the day they carried coloured banners and streamers. There were bands, singers, and tableaux of actors posing on decorated carts. It was all like a great carnival.

At one festival the children came out to test their luck

New Year Festival procession

for the New Year by flying kites. They were not simple things like our kites, but made up in all kinds of fancy shapes; there were birds and dragons and flying tortoises. Usually the strings had bits of broken glass and even small knife-blades knotted into them, and the game was to make the strings cross so that a sharp jerk would cut the other boy's kite string.

There were fireworks, too, with real gunpowder. Even in T'ang times the Chinese had gunpowder, seven hundred years before it was first used in Europe. But in China it was used for sky-rockets and squibs, for crackers and catherine-wheels. In war they sometimes used rockets to scare the enemy, or even to try to set tents on fire, but they were not very effective weapons. The real purpose of these fireworks was to scare away darkness, or to make people happy on great occasions. When eclipses of the sun came, the people would shoot fire-rockets into the sky to scare away the dragon which was trying to eat up the sun.

Religion

Most Chinese were much more interested in luck and bad luck than formal religion. But there were so many of them that there was room for all kinds of opinions.

Most people believed in the Tao, the Power of Heaven and a great number of gods and goddesses who were rather like guardian angels. They all kept the tablets of their ancestors in their homes, and made little offerings once a year to their memory. Most people also studied the wise sayings of Confucius (Kung Fu Tze) who taught how to live a good life among one's neighbours on earth.

A Buddhist priest with shaven head and yellow robe

In T'ang times there were millions of Buddhists in China, and they went on pilgrimages to the places where the Buddha had lived in India. The Buddhists were good-living people, who hoped, by living peaceably and and kindly in this life, to win freedom from being born again into life with all its worries and miseries.

The greatest religious movement from the West in those days was Christianity. Among the caravans of traders from Syria and Persia, there were Nestorian Christian priests who taught of Christ and his death for the redemption of all men. Tai Tsung himself had

The altar of an ancient Chinese church

meetings with the missionaries of the new faith, and he gave them permission to teach and preach in China. He decided that Christianity was not against the rule of Heaven.

The Chinese went to the temples to ask the gods for good luck in their business. Those who could paint words left messages for the temple gods as reminders of what was wanted of them and promises of what would be given to the temples in return.

Writing and Books

Chinese writing began thousands of years ago; at first it was a picture-writing consisting of little scratched pictures of people and animals, made on wood and bone. In later days the signs were changed so that they could be easily written with the Chinese brush and ink. By T'ang times only very clever scholars knew what the pictures had once been before the brush characters had been invented. There were many thousands of these characters. Everyone of them represented a word, and it could be read as a word with the same meaning in any language. In some ways they are like our figures, for instance, 4 can be read as *four* in English, *vier* in German, *cuatro* in Spanish, and so on. The brush-painted words were started on the upper right corner of a page of writing and painted downwards in long columns the whole height of the page. One read downwards and took the columns from right to left: exactly the opposite way to the one we use for our books. The Chinese books were also made up the opposite way from European ones. One has to read a Chinese book from the right-hand page to the left-hand one.

The Chinese had discovered block printing long before T'ang times. They would paint a whole page of

Hand printing from movable blocks of type

a book on thin rice paper, stick it face downwards on a thin slab of wood, and cut away all the surface where there was no painting so that all the letters stood up in relief. Then the board was inked and a sheet of paper pressed on it. When the paper was taken off, the whole page was printed on it. The Chinese were printing books more than eight hundred years before Guttenberg and Caxton began printing in Europe.

Farms and Farmers

Such a great civilisation as the Chinese enjoyed in T'ang times could only exist if there was food enough for the people.

The many small farms were carefully tended by the families who owned them. Every inch of ground was made productive, and was watched over throughout the year.

Every part of China grew its own special crops. The desert towns of the far west grew crops of fine peaches, and produced delicious wines from grapes grown in the few stream valleys. In the south they had the precious ginger plant, and immense forests of bamboo which produced delicate shoots for eating. Peppers and melons, millet grain and precious scented teas; red tea, green tea and black tea were all grown in the southern mountains. On the great swampy plains they grew immense crops of rice, beans and water-lilies. In the northern lands there were also great grain fields, but instead of the rice of the lowlands they grew wheat and barley. There were also huge plantations of soya beans, which produced a fine flour, as well as the dark brown tasty sauce which is so much loved in China.

Most of the little farms of China produced only one or two main crops for market, but the farmer always

Planting out seedlings in
the rice fields

had a full kitchen-garden of pleasant foods for his
family. When there was water near, he bred ducks.
Up on the steppe lands of the north, horse-traders
managed ranches. Fish were bred in special fishponds
in the lowlands. They were farmed very carefully, the
eggs being collected into special tanks. When they
hatched out, the little fish were kept safely in other
tanks for some time before they were released. In this,
the Chinese anticipated modern scientific methods.

In everything the Chinese farmer was careful. He knew the dangers of drought and flood, so he always stored some of the crops he grew in the good years. Fields were manured with a compost of straw, leaves and animal manure. From the towns farmers collected great jars of human manure, which they spread in shallow trenches across their fields. In China nothing was wasted.

The Flowery Land

In T'ang times, China was the most civilised country in all the world. From the careful farmer up to the great Emperor, everyone had work to do for the good of all. Chinese traders spread far afield, and brought goods from Europe, as well as other parts of Asia, into the markets of China. In return they exported magnificent silks and fine pottery.

They respected learning, and believed quite rightly that people should first study the rules of good conduct towards their neighbours. Above all, every Chinese felt that beyond all else there was the unknown Power of Heaven guarding his fate; and that every spring the flowers would bloom after the winter death. That is why they so often called China the Flowery Land, and the Heavenly Empire.

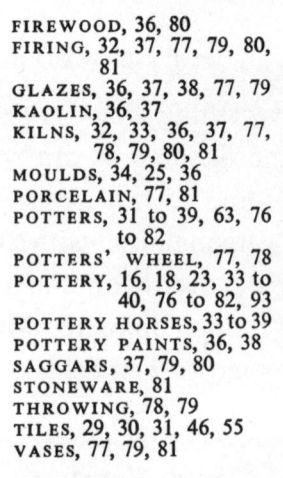

(*Continued from front of book*)

FURNITURE, 21, 74
HALL, 21
HOMES, 11, 12
HOUSEBOATS, 54
HOUSES, 19, 20, 21
MATTRESSES, 23
MIRRORS, 21, 26
OIL, 82
PAINTINGS, 22
PILLOWS, 23, 24
STAIRCASES, 21
TABLES, 21, 22

MUSIC

CYMBALS, 68
DANCERS, 18, 26, 38, 48, 64
DRUMS, 68
FLUTES, 68
GONGS, 68
HORNS, 68
LUTES, 17, 67
MANDOLINES, 67
MUSIC, 17, 65, 66, 67
OBOES, 68
SONG, 17, 18, 85
TAMBOURINES, 68
WIND BELLS, 68
ZITHERS, 67

PEOPLES AND
PLACES

BAGHDAD, 40
CONSTANTINOPLE, 40, 68
CHINA, 7, 8, 27, 40, 41, 57, 62, 93
HUNS, 10
INDIA, 39, 49, 87
INDONESIA, 54
MONGOLS, 41
NANKING, 28, 53
PERSIA, 39, 49, 87
ROME, 51, 68
SYRIA, 49, 87
TARTARS, 10, 41
TIBET, 9, 39, 40
TURKS, 10

POTTERY

CLAY, 31, 35, 36, 77
FIRE BRICKS, 36, 80
FIRECLAY, 35, 36
FIREWOOD, 36, 80
FIRING, 32, 37, 77, 79, 80, 81
GLAZES, 36, 37, 38, 77, 79
KAOLIN, 36, 37
KILNS, 32, 33, 36, 37, 77, 78, 79, 80, 81
MOULDS, 34, 25, 36
PORCELAIN, 77, 81
POTTERS, 31 to 39, 63, 76 to 82
POTTERS' WHEEL, 77, 78
POTTERY, 16, 18, 23, 33 to 40, 76 to 82, 93
POTTERY HORSES, 33 to 39
POTTERY PAINTS, 36, 38
SAGGARS, 37, 79, 80
STONEWARE, 81
THROWING, 78, 79
TILES, 29, 30, 31, 46, 55
VASES, 77, 79, 81

RELIGION

ALTARS, 12, 21, 22, 31
ANCESTORS, 11, 12, 21, 31, 87
ASTROLOGERS, 80
BIBLE, 59
BUDDHISM, 49, 87
CHRISTIANS, 49, 87, 88
CONFUCIUS, 8, 9, 87
DEMONS, 82
DRAGONS, 28, 86
FAIRIES, 68
GODS, 63, 68, 85, 86, 88
HEAVENLY POWER, 56, 57, 86, 93
MAGIC, 27
MOON, 63, 85
NESTORIANS, 49, 87
NEW YEAR, 84
PHOENIX, 28
RELIGION, 34, 38, 41, 53, 56, 63, 68, 80, 82, 85, 86, 87, 88
SPIRITS, 38, 68
TAO, 86
TEMPLES, 63, 85, 88
TORTOISE, 28, 86

TEXTILES

BATIK, 71, 72
BROCADE, 72, 73